STAR

THE STORY OF LITTLE JOHNNY'S RISE TO STARDOM

RAVE BOOKS

In the days before Stardom, he was known as Little Johnny.

Nobody liked him.

Everyone said he was transparent, and had no personality.

And he smelled funny.

All he wanted was to be liked.

To be exciting.

To be a big success.

"Oh to be a great performer," he sighed.

Little Johnny felt so deflated.

He didn't want to see his life go down the pan.

He wanted to be a real mover and shaker.

To sing. To dance. To star at The Dome!

So, off he went to stage school.

"Ok everybody, let's really get those lips moving," said Connie.

Connie Lingus taught the oral classes.

"I'll lick you into shape," she said. "And I'll start with Little Johnny."

Little Johnny swelled with pride and gave her all he had.

"That's the idea," she said. "Feel the rhythm... move with it...go with the flow."

Little Johnny stopped.
"Do you think I'll ever fill The Dome?" he asked.

"Get your act together," she told him.
"And The Dome will be bursting at the seams."

So Connie took Little Johnny in hand.

She worked…

And worked…

And worked him…

Until he was utterly drained.

In bed that night he thought about what Connie had said.

"Practice makes perfect," she'd told him.

"Keep at it. Take it slowly. You'll know when you've got it right."

"Yes," thought Little Johnny. "I'm getting there. I can do it. Yes, Yes, YES!"

Little Johnny felt so much better.

What a relief.

He let out a deep, contented sigh, rolled over and went to sleep.

The next day Little Johnny woke up with a jerk.
(Something he didn't want to do too often.)

He got up and answered the door.

"Hi, I'm May I. Bonkya!" said the voice.

"Wow!" Little Johnny replied in awe.

"I'm going to manage you Little Johnny,"
said the woman who had rung his bell.

"You're playing The Dome tonight!"
she announced.

"But first," she continued, "I've got to see your Performing Entertainer's National Investiture Seal. It's union rules."

"My what?" cried Little Johnny.

"Your P.E.N.I.S. I have to check your P.E.N.I.S. before we go any further," she informed him.

Little Johnny couldn't believe his luck.

May I. Bonkya was the best talent handler in the business.

And here she was wanting to see his P.E.N.I.S.

Without hesitation, Little Johnny showed her.

She smiled sweetly as she took hold,
looked it over, and then gently placed his
P.E.N.I.S. back in its holder.

"That'll do nicely," she said. "I'll fill it out for you
later."

"First let's get down to business, Little Johnny."

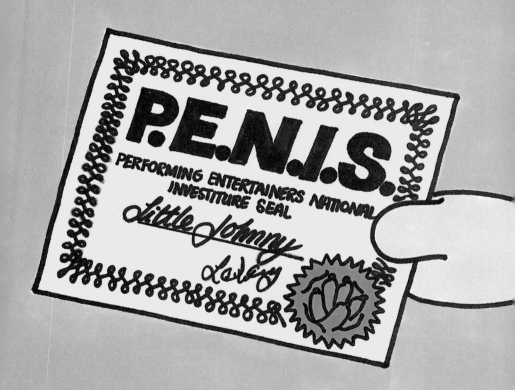

Little Johnny trembled, "It's my first time,
my first real performance – you'll have to guide me."

"Don't worry, I'm here to handle you,"
said May I. Bonkya.

"I'm afraid of being a flop," said Little Johnny.

"I just know you're up to it," she said.

And she handed him a small packet.

"Here, slip this on. You'll perform better in this,
and you'll feel a lot safer."

He opened the packet and squeezed the soft shiny gossamer suit over his head and down the full length of his body.

Gleaming from top to bottom, he really looked ready for action.

"Oh yes!" exclaimed May I. Bonkya. "You look sensational."

"This Little Johnny feels good," he replied.

"Mmmm," she murmured. "You need to be called something else now you're doing The Dome."

"How about The Love Machine?" he asked.

"No," she said. "You're going to shoot to the top – so you shall be known as Stardom."

The Dome was throbbing with excitement.

The stalls were packed tight,

the atmosphere electric...

It was time.

May I. Bonkya nodded in Stardom's direction, "Ready?" she asked.

"OH YES!" said Stardom, and thrust himself into the spotlight.

In the front row he saw a beautiful girl.

He moved towards her.

"*I wanna do it with you Babe...*" he sang.

Her lips glistened, and in the heat
of the moment she was overcome with emotion.

Stardom felt so good. So hot. It was incredible.

The crowd was screaming.

It just got better and better.

The feeling. The rhythm. He was all shook up!

Stardom never wanted to stop.

The Dome was rocking.

Stardom's performance reached its crescendo...

And he showered them with his fantastic finale.

From Little Johnny a star had risen.

Stardom had come!